Uranus

Melissa Stewart

$\mathscr{W}atts$ LIBRARY™

Franklin Watts
A Division of Scholastic Inc.
New York • Toronto • London • Auckland • Sydney
Mexico City • New Delhi • Hong Kong
Danbury, Connecticut

For Bruce

Note to readers: Definitions for words in **bold** can be found in the Glossary at the back of this book.

Photographs © 2002: Corbis Images/Bettmann: 9, 30, 42, 28; Erich Karkoschka: 39; Hulton Archive/Getty Images: 33; NASA: cover, 7, 18, 20, 26, 27, 36 top, 45; NASA/Jet Propulsion Lab Photo: 3, 34 right, 34 left, 37, 50; Photo Researchers, NY: 3, 32 (John Chumack), 19 (Lynette Cook/SPL), 14 (European Space Agency/SPL), 48 (David A. Hardy/SPL), 4 (SPL), 44 (Gianni Tortoli); The Planetary System, Astronomical Society of the Pacific: 36 bottom, 47; Viesti Collection, Inc.: 24 left (Walter Bibikow), 23, 24 right (Joe Viesti).

Solar system diagram created by Greg Harris

The photograph on the cover shows a true-color image of Uranus photographed by *Voyager 2*.

Library of Congress Cataloging-in-Publication Data

Stewart, Melissa.
    Uranus / Melissa Stewart.
        p. cm. — (Watts library)
    Includes bibliographical references and index.
    Summary: Describes the discovery, explorations, atmosphere, orbit, and moons of the seventh planet from the Sun, Uranus.
    ISBN 0-531-12016-3 (lib. bdg.)   0-531-16616-3 (pbk.)
    1. Uranus (Planet)—Juvenile literature. [1. Uranus (Planet)] I. Title. II. Series.

QB681 .S79 2002
523.47—dc21   2001005896

Contents

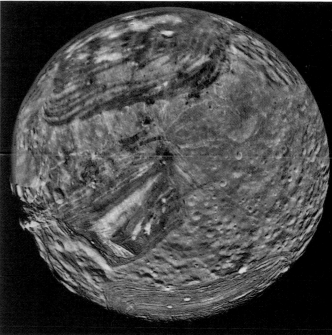

Each night, William Herschel (right) observed the star-filled sky with his homemade telescope. William's sister, Caroline, made notes about what he saw.

Chapter One

A New Planet

During the late 1700s, a self-educated astronomer named William Herschel spent most of his nights observing the star-filled sky. He used a telescope that he had designed and built himself. Whenever he viewed the heavens from his front lawn in Bath, England, William felt excited and peaceful at the same time. The night sky mesmerized him. He wanted to understand all the objects he saw there.

William was born in what is now Hanover, Germany. In 1758, when he was fifteen years old, William fled to England to escape fighting in the Seven

Years' War (1756–1763). Alone and penniless, William struggled to earn a living. Because William's father, a musician and music teacher, had taught all his children about music, William was able to find a job copying musical scores. Later, he too became a music teacher.

In 1766, William was hired as the organist for a church in Bath. Now he was making good money. Instead of working day and night, he could finally devote some time to a new hobby—astronomy. He read dozens of books about astronomy and mathematics, but they did not satisfy his curiosity. He told his sister, Caroline, who had joined him in England, "I resolve to take nothing upon trust, but to see with my own eyes all that other men have seen."

A few days later, William ordered a telescope from a store in London. He spent hours assembling it, only to be disappointed. It was not as powerful as he had hoped. William did not give up his dream of examining all the objects in the night sky, however. Instead, he decided to build his own telescope. Caroline and Alexander, William's brother, were enthusiastic helpers. When the telescope was finished, all three Herschels enjoyed getting a closer look at the stars and planets.

An Amazing Discovery

On a cold, clear evening in mid-March of 1781, William spotted something unusual through his telescope. Most stars appear as a twinkling point of light, but this object looked more like a large, green disk. William was very excited. He thought he had discovered a comet. A few days later, he wrote a paper called *Account of a Comet*.

According to William's report, "On Tuesday the thirteenth March, between ten and eleven in the evening, while I was examining the small stars in the neighborhood of [Gemini], I perceived that one appeared visibly larger than the rest . . . and suspected it to be a comet."

Scientists all over the world began to track the "comet." However, they soon realized that the object was not a comet. It was something much more exciting— a planet. It was the first planet to be discovered in thousands of years. Because all the planets closer to Earth—Mercury, Venus, Mars, Jupiter, and Saturn— are easily visible with the naked eye, they were recognized by stargazers in many ancient civilizations.

The planet that William saw is nearly twice as far from the Sun as Saturn is. Under perfect viewing conditions, it is just barely visible with the naked eye—but only if you know exactly where to look. Discovering this new planet required a

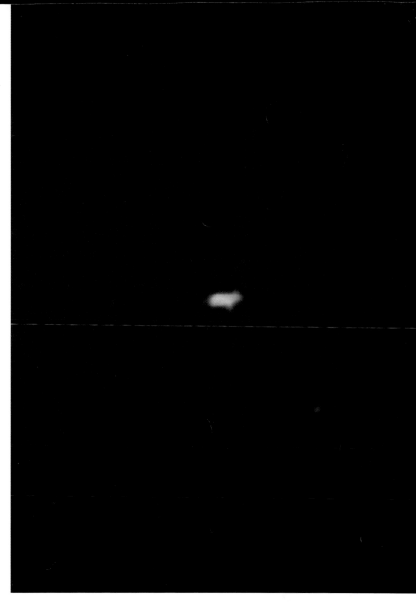

This long-distance Voyager 2 *image is similar to what William Herschel saw through his telescope in 1781.*

telescope, a thorough knowledge of the night sky, and patience. Maybe that is why the planet had been recorded, but mistaken for a star, as many as twenty times before William recognized that it was something special.

Some astronomers were jealous of all the attention William received. Because he did not have a college education, a few scientists even claimed that the discovery was nothing more than dumb luck. William answered these criticisms with the following statement: "It has generally been supposed that a lucky accident brought this [planet] to my view. This is a mistake. In the regular manner that I examined every star in the heavens . . . it was that night its turn to be discovered."

Naming the New Planet

Within a few months, William had learned some basic facts about the new planet. He estimated that it is about four times wider across than Earth. He also calculated that the greenish-blue planet completes one **orbit**, or journey around the Sun, every 84 years.

Naming the new planet took a bit longer. William suggested the name *Georgium Sidus*. These Latin words mean "George's Star." At the time, King George III ruled England, and William wanted to name the planet in his honor. Scientists in other countries objected to this name. Many people thought that the planet should be called Herschel after its discoverer. William was a modest man, however, and he rejected this idea.

All the other planets had names taken from Greek mythology. For example, Mercury was a winged god who carried messages from place to place. Venus was the goddess of beauty, and Mars was the god of war. Jupiter was the king of the gods, and his father was Saturn.

Some astronomers suggested naming the new planet Hypercronus, which means "beyond Saturn," or Cybele, after Saturn's wife. German astronomer Johann Elert Bode proposed the name Uranus. In Greek mythology, Uranus was the father of Saturn and the king of the heavens. Although

German artist Friedrich Schinkel (1781–1841) created this representation of the Greek god Uranus. The painting now hangs in the Old Museum in Berlin, Germany.

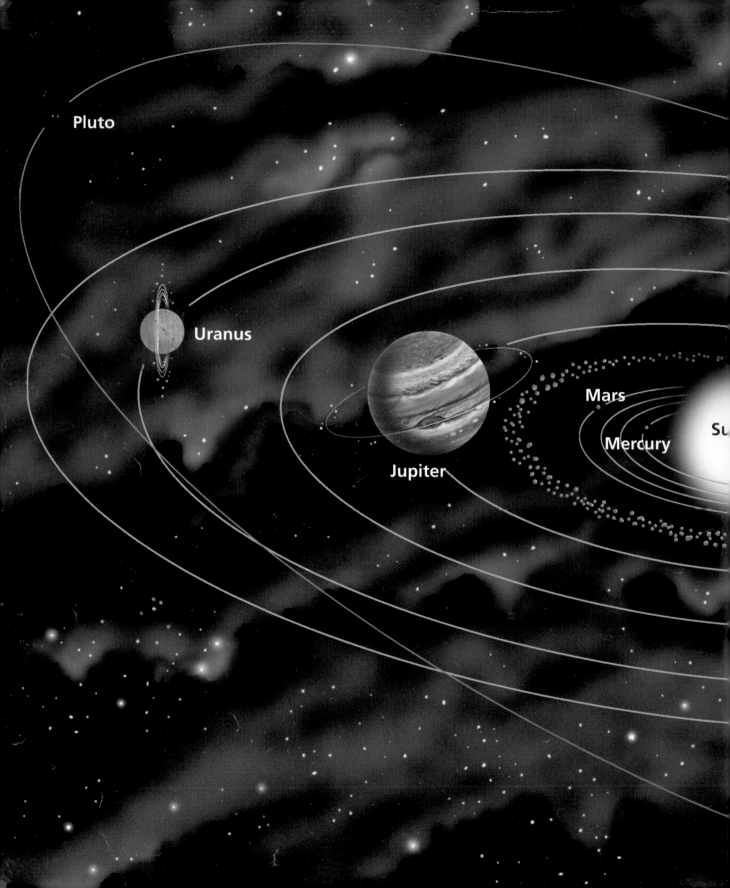

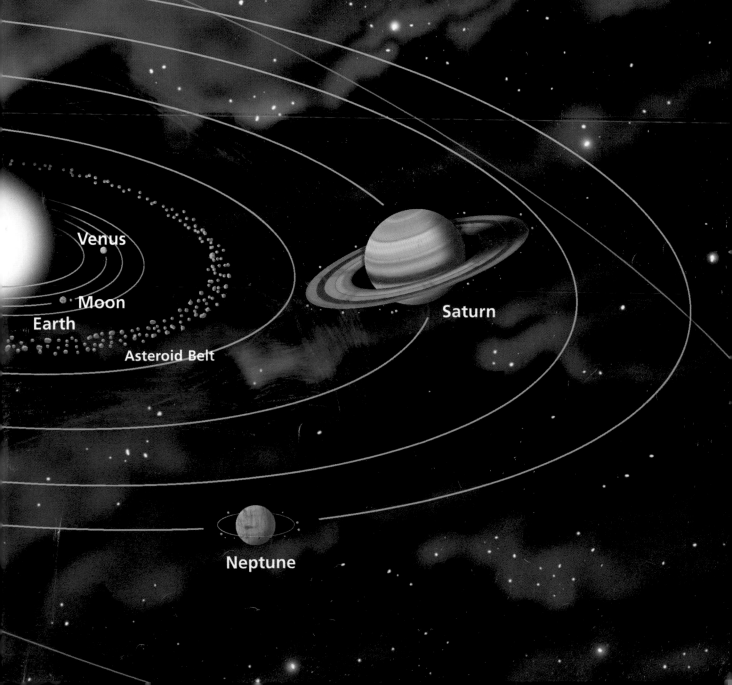

The Solar System

Venus

Moon

Earth

Asteroid Belt

Saturn

Neptune

William approved this name, many astronomers continued to use other names until 1850, when Uranus was universally adopted.

How Uranus Measures Up

Uranus is one of the nine planets that make up our **solar system**. The solar system also includes dozens of moons, comets, **asteroids**, and **meteoroids**. All these objects orbit the Sun. As you can see in the illustration on pages 10 and 11, Uranus is the seventh planet from the Sun.

Uranus is about 1.8 billion miles (2.9 billion kilometers) from the Sun—twenty times farther from the Sun than Earth is. At such a great distance, Uranus receives very little light or heat from the star of our solar system. The average surface temperature on Uranus is a chilly –315 degrees Fahrenheit (–193 degrees Celsius). No life that we know of could survive in such a dark, cold place.

Scientists now know that Uranus is 31,700 miles (51,100 km) across—four times wider than Earth, just as William Herschel predicted. Uranus also has more **mass** than Earth. In other words, Uranus contains a lot more material. Uranus is 14.5 times more massive than Earth.

Modern scientists have also calculated Uranus's **volume**—the total amount of space the planet occupies. Its volume is sixty-seven times greater than Earth's. That means that sixty-seven balls the size of Earth could fit inside Uranus.

Mass and volume are not the only measurements that scientists use to compare planets. They also look at **density**—the relationship between an object's mass and volume. To find a planet's density, all you have to do is divide its mass by its volume. This may seem simple enough, but sometimes the results can be surprising. For example, even though Uranus has more mass and a greater volume than Earth, it is not necessarily more dense.

Imagine that you have two shoeboxes. One is full of feathers, and the other is full of pebbles. It's easy to see that if you have equal volumes of feathers and pebbles, the mass of the pebbles will be much greater, and the density of the pebbles will also be greater. Now imagine that you have a refrigerator box full of feathers and a shoebox full of pebbles. Which do you think is denser? This answer isn't so obvious.

Since Uranus has a greater mass than most other planets, you might expect it to be one of the densest. Don't forget, though, that Uranus also has a greater volume than most other planets. The planet Uranus is similar to a refrigerator box full of feathers, while Earth is similar to a shoebox full of pebbles. It's not so easy to guess which is more dense.

As it turns out, Uranus has a very low density. Earth is about five times denser than Uranus. Why does Uranus have such a low density? Because it is made mostly of gases. That is why scientists call Uranus a gas giant.

Coming in Third

Uranus is huge, but it does not win first prize in our solar system. The largest planet, Jupiter, is 88,800 miles (143,000 km) across. Its mass is 318 times greater than Earth's, and 1,200 balls the size of Earth could fit inside. Saturn, the second-largest planet, is 74,900 miles (120,500 km) across. It is about 95 times more massive than our planet, and 700 balls the size of Earth could fit inside.

In this image of Earth from space, you can see our planet's white ice caps, blue oceans, and greenish-brown surface of Africa.

Chapter Two

A Gas Giant

Have you ever seen a photograph of Earth taken by the Hubble Space Telescope or by astronauts on board the Space Shuttle? At the top and bottom of our globe, you see bright white ice caps. In between, our planet features large areas of shimmering blue ocean and greenish-brown land. Swirling white patches of clouds float far above Earth's surface.

A view of Uranus is not so exciting. When the *Voyager 2* spacecraft flew by Uranus in 1986, all its cameras showed was a large blue-green sphere. Its featureless **atmosphere** seemed boring, and no rocky surface was visible at all.

Magical Methane

Methane is as important on Earth as it is on Uranus. It is the main ingredient of natural gas, which many people use to heat their homes and to cook food.

Uranus is not a solid planet the way Earth is. Uranus is a gas giant—a huge ball of gases and liquids. Jupiter, Saturn, and Neptune are gas giants too. All four planets have deep atmospheres made mostly of hydrogen and helium gas. Uranus's atmosphere is about 3,100 miles (5,000 km) thick. Besides hydrogen and helium, Uranus's atmosphere also contains a small amount of methane gas. Uranus looks blue-green to us because methane reflects these colors.

Gas is very lightweight. Because Uranus has such an immense atmosphere, it has very little mass for its volume. This is why Uranus has such a low density.

Voyage to the Gas Giants

During the 1970s, the National Aeronautics and Space Agency (NASA) sent two pairs of spacecraft to the outer solar system. In 1973, *Pioneer 10* flew by Jupiter. A year later, *Pioneer 11* arrived at Jupiter and then headed on to Saturn. The photographs and data returned to Earth answered many questions, but they also raised many new ones. This led scientists to plan an even more ambitious mission—Voyager.

On September 5, 1977, *Voyager 1* lifted off and flew directly to the outer solar system. It arrived at Jupiter on March 5, 1979, and continued on to Saturn. Finally, it headed for the edge of the solar system. *Voyager 1* captured dozens of images and collected huge quantities of data, but its accomplishments were soon overshadowed by those of its sister spacecraft.

Voyager 2 was launched on August 20, 1977—a few weeks earlier than *Voyager 1*—but it did not reach Jupiter until July 9, 1979. Why did it take so long? Instead of zooming directly to Jupiter, *Voyager 2* took a detour. It was all part of NASA's intricate master plan.

First, *Voyager 2* headed toward the Sun. It swung around Venus and then passed Earth, picking up momentum from the **gravitational fields** of both planets. The spacecraft needed this extra boost so that it could do something very special—visit Uranus and Neptune.

NASA had planned *Voyager 2*'s flight to coincide with a planetary line-up that occurs only once every 189 years. As a result, *Voyager 2* was able to fly by all four gas giants. At each planet, *Voyager 2* received an additional "**gravity** assist," which helped propel the spacecraft to its next target.

Voyager 2 passed by Uranus on January 24, 1986. It is the only spacecraft that has ever visited the blue-green planet. The thousands of photographs it took helped scientists identify five of the planet's rings and ten of its moons. Other

What Happened to the Voyagers?

After completing their primary missions, *Voyager 1* and *Voyager 2* continued to zoom through space. By early 2001, *Voyager 1* was more than 7.5 billion miles (12 billion km) from Earth, while *Voyager 2* was more than 6 billion miles (9.4 billion km) away. The spacecraft may reach the edge of the solar system by 2003. They have enough fuel to continue operating until about 2020.

A computer-generated representation of **Voyager 2** *approaching Uranus*

equipment on board the spacecraft recorded the planet's temperature and helped scientists understand what Uranus is like deep inside.

Inside Uranus

Far below the surface, Uranus has a sizzling-hot, slushy ocean made of water, methane, and ammonia. On Earth, water boils, or **evaporates**, at 212°F (100°C), but the water in Uranus's ocean has a temperature of 12,000°F (6,650°C). How is this possible? Temperature is not the only factor that determines whether a material exists as a solid, a liquid, or a gas. **Pressure** also plays a role.

All the gases in Uranus's giant atmosphere press against the ocean, so the pressure at the top of the ocean is about five million times greater than the pressure that Earth's thin atmosphere exerts on its oceans, lakes, and rivers. The tremendous pressure of gases on Uranus holds the **molecules** that make up its ocean so close together that they cannot evaporate and become a gas.

At its very center, Uranus might have a small rocky core. Some scientists estimate that this core is about 2,480 miles (4,000 km) across.

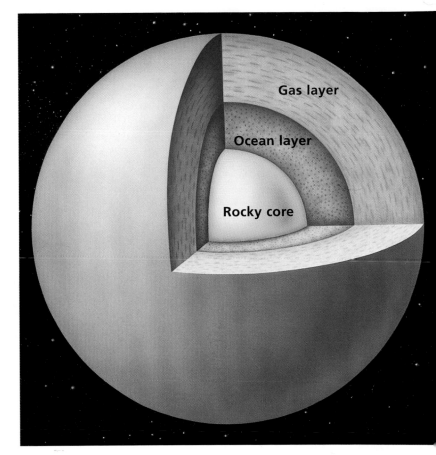

Gas layer

Ocean layer

Rocky core

Scientists believe Uranus has three layers. The outermost gassy layer surrounds a hot, slushy ocean. Deep inside, the planet may have a rocky core about the size of Earth's Moon.

This dramatic image of *Uranus* was recorded by **Voyager 2** *as the spacecraft moved away from the planet.*

Chapter Three

Tipped on Its Side

Since Uranus was discovered in 1781, it has traveled around the Sun about two and a half times. During the same period, Earth has completed more than two hundred orbits. Because Earth is much closer to the Sun than Uranus is, our planet takes just 365 days—or 1 year—to make the journey.

A year is the amount of time it takes for a planet to **revolve**, or circle, around the Sun once. This means that the length of a year is different on each planet. The farther a planet is from the Sun, the longer its year lasts. Just as William Herschel estimated, a year on Uranus is about 30,660 Earth-days—or 84 Earth-years—long.

Uranus and all the other planets in the solar system revolve around the Sun because they are trapped by a powerful but invisible force called gravity. Just as the Sun's gravity tugs on planets, asteroids, comets, and meteoroids, Earth's gravity pulls on the Moon. It also pulls ripe apples, winter snowflakes, and whizzing baseballs toward the ground.

Earth is not the only planet with a gravitational field. Uranus has its own gravitational field, and so does every other object in space. The greater an object's mass, the stronger its gravitational pull. Since Uranus is much more massive than Earth, its gravitational pull is much stronger—strong enough to keep at least twenty moons and eleven rings endlessly circling the planet.

A Strange Spin

As Uranus orbits the Sun, it also **rotates**, or turns on its **axis**—an imaginary line through the center of a planet. During each rotation, material near Uranus's **equator** must travel farther than material near its poles. To understand how this works, imagine a marching band turning a corner. The musicians on the outside edge of the band have farther to travel than musicians closest to the corner. For the band to move as a group, the musicians on the outside edge must take large steps while musicians on the inside edge take very small steps. Similarly,

material near Uranus's equator must move faster than material at its poles.

It's easy for a band member to adjust the size of his or her steps, but it isn't so easy for different areas of a planet to move at different speeds. **Inertia**—the tendency of a still object to stay at rest, and a moving object to continue moving—draws the fast-moving material near the equator away from the planet in a straight line. At the same time, gravity pulls the material toward the center of the

As the Scottsville Clown Band turns a corner, the musicians on the right side of this photo take large steps, while musicians on the left take small steps. Because Uranus cannot make the same kind of adjustments as it orbits the Sun, it bulges at the equator and flattens at the poles.

When it is daytime in Paris, France, the Sun lights the Eiffel Tower (left). At night, the Sun is shining on the opposite side of the world, so electricity is used to light up the Eiffel Tower (right).

planet. If you look closely at Uranus, you can see evidence of this internal tug-of-war. It is what makes the planet bulge slightly at the equator and flatten at the poles.

Most planets spin on their axes like toy tops. Earth rotates once every 23 hours and 56 minutes. That is the length of a day on our planet. As long as you stay in one part of the world, you will experience daytime when your half of Earth is facing toward the Sun and nighttime when your half of Earth is facing away from the Sun. During a year, you experience 365 days and 365 nights. As Earth moves around the Sun, you also experience spring, summer, autumn, and winter.

Things are different on Uranus. Compared to the other planets, Uranus is tipped on its side. It spins more like a bicycle wheel than a toy top. To see the difference, look back at the diagram of the solar system on pages 10 and 11. Try to imagine where each planet's axis would be.

Uranus completes one spin every 17 hours and 14 minutes. That is the length of a day on Uranus. But that day is not divided into a bright, sunny daytime and a pitch-black nighttime as it is on Earth. Instead, it is more correct to say that every part of the great blue-green world experiences a 42-year season of light and a 42-year season of darkness as Uranus completes each 84-year journey around the Sun.

Scientists are not sure why Uranus has such an unusual tilt. Some researchers suspect that a very large object crashed into the planet billions of years ago. The collision would not have destroyed the hardy planet, but the force of the impact could have knocked Uranus onto its side.

Seasons on Uranus

The Sun shines directly over each of Uranus's poles for nearly one-quarter of each year. Although half the planet is dark for long periods of time, the dark half remains at about the same temperature as the sunny half. Even though Uranus's poles get more sunlight than its equator does, the equator is always the

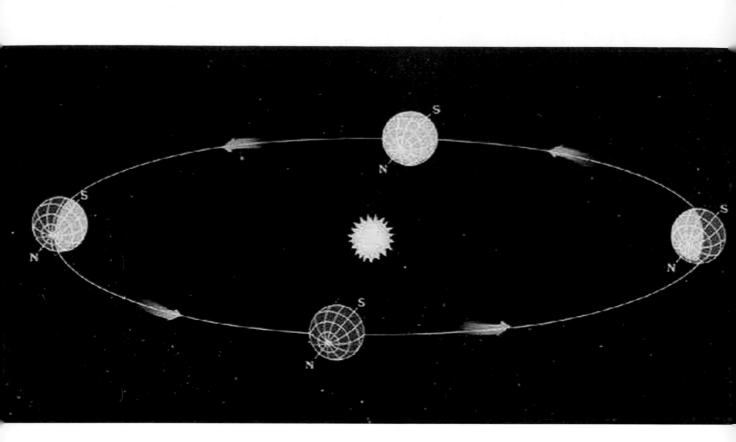

Because Uranus is tipped on its side, each pole receives direct sunlight for one-quarter of the year.

warmest area of the planet. Scientists do not know how to explain this.

When *Voyager 2* flew by Uranus in 1986, the planet's south pole was pointed almost directly at the Sun. As a result, the planet's southern hemisphere was in the midst of a sunny summer and the northern hemisphere was experiencing a long, dark winter. By 2007, the Sun will be directly over Uranus's equator. Spring will have arrived in the northern hemisphere, while the southern hemisphere will be entering autumn.

Recent photographs taken by the Hubble Space Telescope (HST) suggest that Uranus might not always be as smooth and featureless as it was when *Voyager 2* visited in 1986. As the

The Hubble Space Telescope

In 1990, NASA launched the school bus–sized Hubble Space Telescope (HST) into orbit around Earth. Scientists were disappointed by its first images, but soon realized that the telescope's main mirror was flawed.

In 1993, astronauts aboard the Space Shuttle *Discovery* repaired HST. Photographs taken since then have answered many scientists' questions about objects inside and outside our solar system, and have also raised many new questions. Additional Space Shuttle repair missions in 1997, 1999, and 2001 have helped keep the telescope working properly.

The Hubble Space Telescope's infrared camera recorded this image of Uranus on August 14, 1994. The bright spot in the planet's southern hemisphere is a band of clouds.

northern hemisphere reawakens from its winter hibernation, the planet's atmosphere seems to be coming alive. About halfway between Uranus's north pole and equator, winds blow at speeds of up to 360 miles (575 km) per hour. Closer to the equator, 225-mile-per-hour (360-km-per-hour) winds gust in the opposite direction.

HST has had better luck than *Voyager 2* in viewing activity in Uranus's atmosphere because it has a special infrared camera. Images from this camera have revealed that Uranus has bands of clouds just like those in the more colorful atmosphere of Jupiter.

Uranus's Magnetic Field

Besides a gravitational field, Uranus also has a **magnetic field**. A planet's magnetic field is similar to the magnetic field around the magnets that many people stick on their refrigerators. If you hold a magnet close to your refrigerator, you can feel the pull, or attraction, between the two objects. If you hold the magnet a little farther away, you will not feel the same pull because the refrigerator is now outside the magnet's magnetic field.

The magnetic field surrounding a planet is much stronger than the one around any magnet that you can hold in your hand. Uranus is not the only planet with a magnetic field. Mercury, Earth, Jupiter, and Saturn do too. As these planets orbit the Sun, long, invisible magnetic "tails" stretch out behind them. Uranus's magnetic tail extends at least 6.2 million miles (10 million km) out into space.

We cannot see the magnetic tails of planets, but we can detect them in other ways. Images created from data collected from spacecraft and observers on Earth show that the shape of most magnetic fields is similar to the gassy tail of a comet. Uranus's twisted tail is shaped more like a spiraling corkscrew. Scientists are not sure why this is the case.

King George III
ruled England from
1760 until his death
in 1820.

Chapter Four

The Moons of Uranus

About a year after William Herschel discovered Uranus, King George III sent word that he would like to meet the talented amateur astronomer. William was honored, but very nervous about meeting such a powerful ruler.

King George congratulated William and told him that his discovery of Uranus had brought respect to England. To help William continue his work, King George began paying him a generous annual salary. William was thrilled. Now he

What a Coincidence!

William Hershel was born in 1738 and died in 1822, when he was eighty-four years old. During William's lifetime, Uranus made one complete journey around the Sun.

could devote all his time to astronomy. Although he spent many, many hours studying stars, every now and then William pointed his telescope toward Uranus.

In 1787, as William observed his favorite planet, he noticed two tiny objects very close to Uranus. As he continued to watch the dots of light, he realized that they were orbiting the blue-green planet. He had discovered two moons around Uranus! William named the moons Oberon and Titania, after the king and queen of the fairies in William Shakespeare's famous play *A Midsummer Night's Dream*.

In 1851, British astronomer William Lassell detected two more moons around Uranus. He called them Ariel and Umbriel, after two fairies in the popular poem *The Rape of the Lock* by British poet and essayist Alexander Pope. Another moon, Miranda, was spotted in 1948 by American astronomer

At the center of this image, Oberon and Titania can be seen orbiting Uranus.

Gerard Peter Kuiper. Its name was taken from a character in *The Tempest*, another play by Shakespeare.

Scientists now know that Uranus has at least twenty moons. Most researchers believe that many others are still waiting to be discovered. In fact, one additional moon spotted in 1999 might receive an official name very soon.

The Big Moons of Uranus

It is no big surprise that Oberon, Titania, Ariel, Umbriel, and Miranda were the first Uranian moons discovered. They are all large and orbit fairly close to the planet. Like Earth's moon, they are rocky, solid objects covered with craters—large depressions that show where they have been struck by objects plummeting through space.

Titania, the largest moon, takes about 8 Earth-days to complete one trip around Uranus. Long, deep grooves on the moon's surface might have been made by a comet that crash-landed on the moon three or four billion years ago. Other features on Titania suggest that soft, hot, rocky material from deep within the moon might once have risen to the surface, spewed in every direction, and then frozen. Some scientists believe that Titania is still active. They see evidence of recent earthquakes on Uranus's largest moon.

Oberon is a bit smaller than its neighbor Titania. Made of ice and rock, this light-colored moon takes about 13 days to

In this 1945 production of A Midsummer Night's Dream, *Oberon (left) was played by famous British actor John Gielgud. Titania (right) was played by Peggy Ashcroft.*

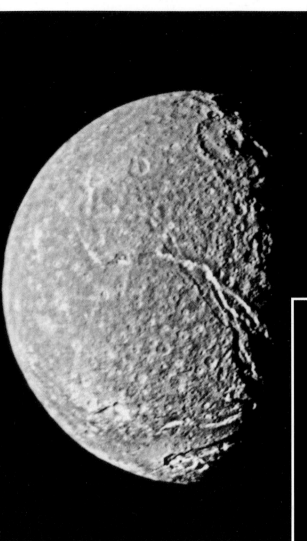

circle Uranus. It has high mountains and deep valleys, suggesting that its crust has moved, fractured, and folded over time. Some of Oberon's deep craters might once have been flooded with dark fluid that welled up from deep inside the moon. Now the fluid is frozen solid, and the moon seems inactive.

Voyager 2 *recorded these images of* Titania *(above) and* Oberon *(right) in 1986.*

Moons of Uranus

Name	Distance from Uranus	Distance Across	Year of Discovery
Cordelia	30,910 miles (49,750 km)	16 miles (26 km)	1986
Ophelia	33,400 miles (53,160 km)	19 miles (30 km)	1986
Bianca	36,760 miles (59,160 km)	26 miles (42 km)	1986
Cressida	38,390 miles (61,780 km)	39 miles (62 km)	1986
Desdemona	38,940 miles (62,660 km)	34 miles (54 km)	1986
Juliet	39,990 miles (64,360 km)	52 miles (84 km)	1986
Portia	41,070 miles (66,100 km)	67 miles (108 km)	1986
Rosalind	43,450 miles (69,930 km)	34 miles (54 km)	1986
S/1986 U10*	46,610 miles (75,000 km)	25 miles (40 km)	1999
Belinda	46,760 miles (75,260 km)	41 miles (66 km)	1986
Puck	53,440 miles (86,000 km)	96 miles (154 km)	1985
Miranda	80,640 miles (129,780 km)	301 miles (485 km)	1948
Ariel	118,800 miles (191,240 km)	721 miles (1,160 km)	1851
Umbriel	165,300 miles (265,970 km)	739 miles (1,190 km)	1851
Titania	270,800 miles (435,840 km)	1,000 miles (1,610 km)	1787
Oberon	362,000 miles (582,600 km)	963 miles (1,550 km)	1787
Caliban	4,455,000 miles (7,169,000 km)	37 miles (60 km)†	1997
Stephano	4,940,000 miles (7,948,000 km)	25 miles (40 km)†	1999
Sycorax	7,589,000 miles (12,214,000 km)	75 miles (120 km)†	1997
Prospero	10,297,000 miles (16,568,000 km)	25 miles (40 km)†	1999
Setebos	10,989,000 miles (17,681,000 km)	25 miles (40 km)†	1999

* This moon must be confirmed before it can receive an official name.

† Approximate distances across

Ariel (above) and Umbriel (below) are similar in size but have very different surface features.

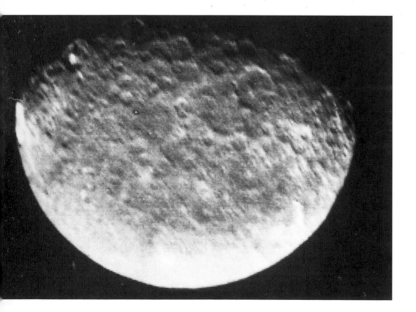

Uranus's largest moons seem to come in pairs. Just as Titania and Oberon are similar in size, so are Ariel and Umbriel. The surfaces of these two moons are quite different, however. Ariel has wide, curving valleys, smooth plains, and twisted canyons. Bright circles mark the locations of icy crater rims. Long faults that crisscross the moon's surface suggest an active past. Like Oberon, forces deep within Ariel have changed its surface over time.

Umbriel is dark and almost featureless. It appears to have changed very little since it formed billions of years ago. Like the other large moons, Umbriel's craters show that it has been struck thousands of times. A white patch near the moon's equator has been given the name Wunda, but scientists do not know what it is. Some researchers think it might be a new crater with a freshly exposed icy exterior that reflects light from the Sun.

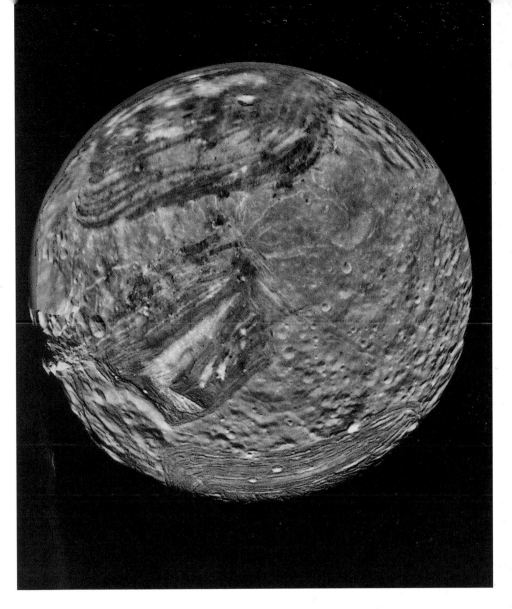

Miranda is the smallest of Uranus's large moons, and perhaps the most mysterious. Imagine what would happen if you dropped a ceramic dish on the kitchen floor, and it shattered into a dozen pieces. As you tried to glue all those pieces back together, you accidentally put a few in the wrong place. Then the glue dried before you noticed your mistakes. That dish would look similar to Miranda.

Scientists believe that long ago, a giant object smashed into Miranda and broke it apart. When the force of their own gravity pulled the pieces back together, they got all mixed up. Miranda's jumbled surface is a hodgepodge of cliffs, canyons, cracks, and craters.

Some areas of Miranda's surface look like they have been lifted and twisted, rippled and bent to form huge ovals with names like Alonso and Stephano and a deep V called Chevron. One of the moon's strangest features is the "racetrack"—a series of large, circular grooves near the equator. Each "groove" is actually a valley ten times deeper than the Grand Canyon.

The Eleven Inner Moons

Uranus is twenty times farther from the Sun than Earth is, and it receives about four hundred times less sunlight than our planet does. Uranus's neighborhood is a dark place, so it's no wonder that viewers on Earth have trouble seeing small objects near the planet. For many years, scientists had suspected that Uranus had more than five moons, and photos from *Voyager 2* proved that they were right.

In 1985, while the spacecraft was still thousands of miles from Uranus, *Voyager 2*'s cameras spied tiny Puck—a moon just 96 miles (154 km) across. As the spacecraft closed in on Uranus, it returned photos that clearly showed nine more small, dark-colored moons orbiting close to the giant planet. According to the tradition begun by William Herschel and

William Lassell, all of their names came from works written by Shakespeare or Pope. They are Cordelia, Ophelia, Bianca, Cressida, Desdemona, Juliet, Portia, Rosalind, and Belinda.

In 1999, Erich Karkoschka, a researcher at the University of Arizona's Lunar and Planetary Lab, was comparing images taken by *Voyager 2* and the Hubble Space Telescope when he noticed something surprising—a new moon. Karkoschka was amazed, and so were other scientists. "This discovery is very unusual," Karkoschka told reporters. "Typically, moons are found within days after the discovery image has been taken. In this case, the discovery image is more than thirteen years old."

Erich Karkoschka discovered Uranus's eighteenth moon in 1999.

The new moon, known as S/1986 U10, is similar to the other moons that *Voyager 2* captured on film—small and close to Uranus. Karkoschka thinks this moon is about 25 miles (40 km) across and completes one orbit every 15 hours and 18 minutes.

Five More Moons

If you've been keeping count, you probably think that S/1986 U10 is Uranus's sixteenth moon. Actually, though, it's number eighteen. The sixteenth and seventeenth moons were discovered by Canadian astronomer Brett Gladman and American astronomer Philip Nicholson in 1997. At the

What's in a Name?

Whenever someone spots a new object in the night sky, the International Astronomical Union assigns it a temporary name until scientists confirm that the object has not already been identified. For now, the moon Erich Karkoschka found is being called S/1986 U10. How did the moon get this name? It is the tenth previously unknown satellite (S), or moon, of Uranus (U10), and it was spotted in 1986. Even though Karkoschka did not notice the moon until 1999, it first appeared in a photograph taken by *Voyager 2* in 1986.

time, the scientists were examining a series of photographs they had just taken with a camera attached to a 200-inch (508-centimeter) telescope at the Palomar Observatory on Mount Palomar in California.

These newly discovered moons, Caliban and Sycorax, are very different from Uranus's other moons. Joseph Burns, a professor of engineering and astronomy at Cornell University, describes them as "irregular lumps of dark ice and gunk." Each moon orbits more than 4 million miles (7 million km) away from Uranus. Also, while the planet's big moons and inner moons all travel from east to west around Uranus, Caliban and Sycorax travel from west to east. In other words, they orbit backward.

In 1999, not long after Erich Karkoschka discovered S/1986 U10, the team of scientists working at Palomar Observatory spotted three more moons orbiting millions of miles from the blue-green planet. Like Caliban and Sycorax, the new moons are moving backward. It didn't take long to prove that these objects had not previously been identified. As a result, they have recently been given the names Stephano, Prospero, and Setebos. Scientists believe that all five distant moons might once have been asteroids that became trapped by Uranus's giant gravitational field when their orbits took them too close to the mighty planet.

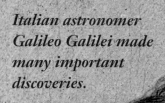

Italian astronomer Galileo Galilei made many important discoveries.

Chapter Five

Rings Around Uranus

In the early 1600s—long before William Herschel noticed Uranus—an Italian scientist named Galileo Galilei made an important discovery of his own. Like William, Galileo used a telescope that he had built himself.

When Galileo looked at Saturn, he noticed strange bulges on either side of the planet's round disk. Galileo called these bulges "ears," but he could not explain them. Using a more powerful telescope, Dutch astronomer Christian

Galileo's first telescope

TVBVM OPTICVM VIDES GALILAEI ... NTVM, ET OPVS, QVO SOLIS MACVLAS,
ET E ... NAE MONTES, ET ... S SATELLITES, ET NOVAM QVASI

Named in Their Honor

The *Cassini-Huygens*, a space-craft that will arrive at Saturn in 2004, is named after Giovanni Domenico Cassini and Christian Huygens. The Cassini orbiter will make seventy loops around the planet, while the Huygens probe will drop to the surface of Titan, Saturn's largest moon.

Huygens saw these "ears" more clearly. He suggested that Saturn is encircled by a ring of material. About twenty years later, in 1675, French-Italian astronomer Giovanni Domenico Cassini realized that Saturn has at least two rings. Finally, more than three hundred years later, the Voyager spacecraft showed scientists that Saturn has seven separate rings.

William Herschel knew all about the work of Galileo, Huygens, and Cassini. He, too, observed Saturn's rings through his telescope. He even discovered two of Saturn's moons—Mimas and Enceladus. William never imagined,

Rings of Uranus

Name	Distance from Uranus	Width
1986U2R	23,620 miles (38,000 km)	1,550 miles (2,500 km)
6	26,000 miles (41,840 km)	0.6 to 1.9 miles (1 to 3 km)
5	26,250 miles (42,230 km)	1.3 to 1.9 miles (2 to 3 km)
4	26,460 miles (42,580 km)	1.3 to 1.9 miles (2 to 3 km)
Alpha	27,790 miles (44,720 km)	4.4 to 7.5 miles (7 to 12 km)
Beta	28,380 miles (45,670 km)	4.4 to 7.5 miles (7 to 12 km)
Eta	29,330 miles (47,190 km)	Up to 1.3 miles (2 km)
Gamma	29,600 miles (47,630 km)	0.6 to 2.5 miles (1 to 4 km)
Delta	30,010 miles (48,290 km)	1.9 to 5.6 miles (3 to 9 km)
1986U1R	31,090 miles (50,020 km)	0.6 to 1.3 miles (1 to 2 km)
Epsilon	31,780 miles (51,140 km)	12.4 to 62.2 miles (20 to 100 km)

however, that Uranus might have rings of its own—and neither did anyone else until 1977.

On March 10, 1977, a team of scientists noticed that a star flickered strangely just before Uranus moved in front of it. On a hunch, American astronomer James L. Elliot, the team's leader, asked another group of scientists to look for a similar irregularity when the star reappeared. Sure enough, they

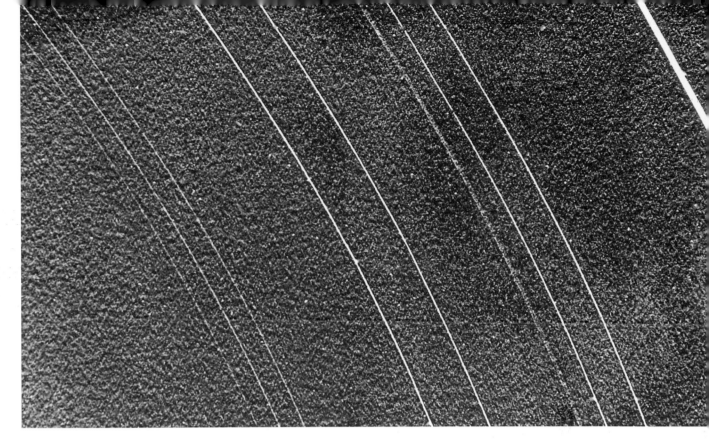

observed the same kind of flickering activity. Something just beyond Uranus must be blocking some of the star's light. The only possible explanation was that the planet had rings—at least five of them. Today, we know these five rings as Alpha, Beta, Gamma, Delta, and Epsilon.

During the next decade, additional observations from Earth revealed four more rings, bringing the new total to nine. When *Voyager 2* visited Uranus in 1986, it returned images that helped scientists confirm the first nine rings and identify two more—1986U1R and 1986U2R. The spacecraft also spotted some partial rings, or arcs, as well as a variety of ringlets and broad bands of fine dust orbiting the blue-green planet.

This image of Uranus's nine rings was recorded by Voyager 2.

Rings of Ice and Dust

If you look at Saturn through a backyard telescope on a clear night, you will be able to see its brightly glimmering rings. You will not be able to see Jupiter's rings—even though they are closer to Earth. This is because Saturn's rings are made of ice chunks that reflect sunlight, while Jupiter's rings are made of tiny particles of dark dust.

Uranus's rings are made mostly of beachball-sized ice chunks. They do not reflect light as Saturn's rings do, however. In fact, they are as black as coal. Some scientists think the

An artist's representation of the dark objects that make up Uranus's rings

ice might be coated with the same dark dust that orbits Uranus in broad belts.

Scientists think that Uranus's rings formed much more recently than the planet. Uranus and the other planets in our solar system are about 4.6 billion years old, but Uranus's rings probably formed no more than 100 million years ago. As the planet's moons collided with or were struck by meteoroids, some rocky material broke off. Gravity trapped these bits and pieces to create rings.

Shepherds in the Sky

When *Voyager 2* visited Uranus's neighborhood, it recorded many images of Epsilon, the planet's brightest, outermost ring. Some images showed that two moons, Cordelia and Ophelia, orbit on either side of Epsilon. When scientists studied images from Saturn, they noticed that three of its rings were also flanked by moons. Was this just a coincidence? Researchers didn't think so.

Scientists now believe that moons "shepherd" many—or possibly even all—planetary rings. The moons' gravitational pulls keep ring particles organized as they move around a planet. Just as a shepherd keeps his or her animals in a tight herd, shepherd moons orbit close to the edges of a ring and prevent the materials from straying.

If this theory is true, it is likely that Uranus and the other gas giants have many more moons that no one has detected yet. Although scientists continue to look for more shepherd

Saturn's Shepherds

Scientists consider six of Saturn's moons to be shepherds. They are Pan, Atlas, Pandora, Prometheus, Epimetheus, and Janus.

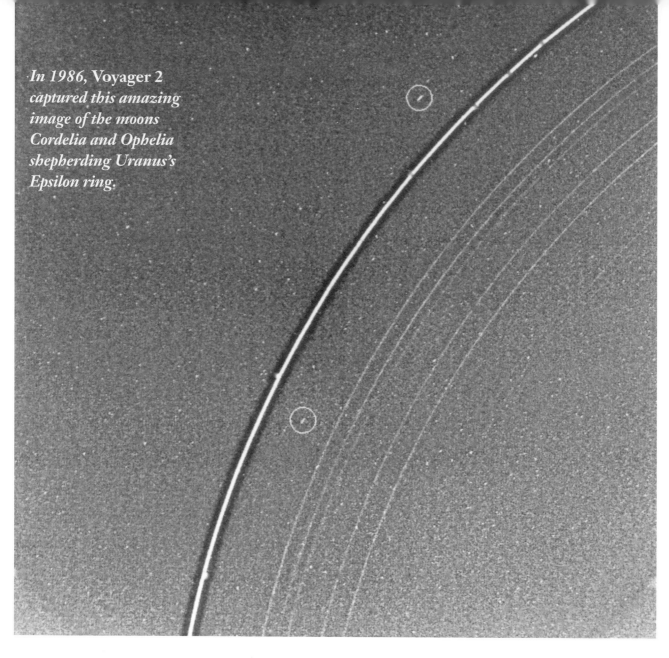

In 1986, Voyager 2 captured this amazing image of the moons Cordelia and Ophelia shepherding Uranus's Epsilon ring.

moons, their location so close to the rings—and to the giant planets—would make them difficult to spot. Still, the search continues.

Perhaps one day, another spacecraft will travel to Uranus. It might help scientists find more moons. It could also help researchers answer many of their other questions about the great blue-green planet. They would like to know more about the planet's mysterious interior ocean and find out whether Uranus really does have a rocky core. They would also like to learn more about the weather and seasons on this strange, tipped-over world. For now, though, researchers continue to study images and data from *Voyager 2*. They, too, may still have secrets to share.

Glossary

asteroid—a chunk of rock left over from the formation of the solar system. Most asteroids orbit the Sun in a belt between Mars and Jupiter.

atmosphere—the gases that surround a planet or other body in space

axis—the imaginary line running from pole to pole through a planet's center. A planet spins, or rotates, along its axis.

comet—a small ball of rock and ice that orbits the Sun. When it gets close to the Sun, some of the ice melts and releases gases and dust particles that form a tail.

density—an object's mass divided by its volume

equator—an imaginary line running around the center of a planet, halfway between the poles

evaporate—to change from a liquid to a gas

gravitational field—the volume of space affected by a planet's gravity

gravity—the force that pulls two objects toward each other, such as a moon toward a planet

inertia—the tendency of an object at rest to stay at rest and an object in motion to stay in motion

magnetic field—the area surrounding a magnet that is affected by the magnet's attractive force. Some planets have magnetic properties and, therefore, have a magnetic field.

mass—the amount of matter or material in an object

meteoroid—a small rocky or metallic object that was once part of a comet or asteroid

molecule—a group of atoms that form the smallest unit of a substance that can exist and retain its chemical properties

nebula (pl. **nebulae**)—a primitive cloud of gases and dust from which the Sun and the planets were born

orbit—to move around another object; to revolve

pressure—a force that one object exerts on another

revolve—to move around another object; to orbit

rotate—to spin on an axis

solar system—a group of planets that orbit around a central star

volume—the total amount of space that an object occupies

To Find
Out More

Books

Apfel, Necia. *Voyager to the Planets*. New York: Clarion, 1991.

Campbell, Ann Jeanette. *The New York Public Library Amazing Space: A Book of Answers for Kids*. New York: John Wiley & Sons, 1997.

Hartmann, William K. and Don Miller. *The Grand Tour: A Traveler's Guide to the Solar System*. New York: Workman, 1993.

Scott, Elaine. *Adventure in Space: The Flight to Fix the Hubble Space Telescope*. New York: Hyperion, 1995.

Online Sites

NASA Ask the Space Scientist

http://image.gsfc.nasa.gov/poetry/ask/askmag.html#list

Take a look at the Interactive Page where NASA scientists answer your questions about astronomy, space, and space missions. The site also has access to archives and fact sheets.

NASA Newsroom

http://www.nasa.gov/newsinfo/newsroom.html

This site features NASA's latest press releases, status reports, and fact sheets. It includes a news archive with past reports and a search button for the NASA Web site. You can even sign up for e-mail versions of all NASA press releases.

The Nine Planets: A Multimedia Tour of the
Solar System

http://www.seds.org/nineplanets/nineplanets/nineplanets.html

This site has excellent material on the planets, including Uranus. It was created and is maintained by the Students for the Exploration and Development of Space, University of Arizona.

Planetary Missions

http://nssdc.gsfc.nasa.gov/planetary/projects.html

At this site, you will find NASA links to all their current and past missions.

Welcome to the Planets

http://pds.jpl.nasa.gov/planets/

This tour of the solar system has lots of pictures and information. The site was created and is maintained by the California Institute of Technology for NASA/Jet Propulsion Laboratory.

Windows to the Universe

http://windows.arc.nasa.gov/

This NASA site, developed by the University of Michigan, includes sections on "Our Planet," "Our Solar System," "Space Missions," and "Kids' Space." Choose from presentation levels of beginner, intermediate, or advanced.

Places to Visit

Drefus Planetarium
49 Washington Street
P.O. Box 540
Newark, NJ 07101

Exploratorium
3601 Lyon Street
San Francisco, CA 94123

Hansen Planetarium
15 South State Street
Salt Lake City, UT 84111

Howell Observatory
1400 W. Mars Hill Road
Flagstaff, AZ 86001

Miami Space Transit Planetarium
3280 South Miami Avenue
Miami, FL 33129

National Air and Space Museum
7th and Independence Avenue SW
Washington, DC 20560

Space Center Houston
1601 NASA Road One
Houston, TX 77058

A Note on Sources

I have written other books and magazine articles about space, so I knew a little bit about Uranus before I began my research. Still, I thought it was best to start with the basics. To learn about the planet's most important characteristics, I visited my local library and read several encyclopedia entries about Uranus.

Then I read a variety of recent articles from magazines and scientific journals. I also looked at the photos and information available on several Web sites created and maintained by the National Aeronautics and Space Agency (NASA). Scientists are learning more about space every day, and I wanted to make sure that this book would discuss all the most recent findings. Whenever possible, I spoke directly with the scientists who made recent discoveries and included quotations from them.

Next, I reviewed a variety of children's books about Uranus. I wanted to know what other people were writing, so

I could find ways to make this book unique. I discovered that most other books spend very little time discussing the tremendous contributions of William and Caroline Herschel. I read several biographies of the brother-and-sister astronomy team and included several direct quotations from William. In the end, my goal was to breathe life into the text by combining the important scientific facts with the excitement of discovery.

—*Melissa Stewart*

Index

Numbers in *italics* indicate illustrations.

63

About the Author

Melissa Stewart was just six months old when the first astronauts walked on the Moon. Her parents knew it was a monumental occasion and took dozens of pictures of her watching the event on television.

As the child of a medical scientist and an engineer, Stewart grew up surrounded by science. She soon developed her own love of the natural world and the faraway worlds she could see in the night sky.

After earning a degree in biology from Union College and a master's degree in science journalism from New York University, Stewart spent a decade working as an editor before becoming a full-time writer. She has written more than two dozen children's books about animals, ecosystems, earth science, and space science. Three of these titles—*Life Without Light: A Journey to Earth's Dark Ecosystems*; *Seals, Sea Lions, and Walruses*; and *Science in Ancient China*—were published by Franklin Watts. Stewart lives in Marlborough, Massachusetts.